The Book of Things

Other Books by Russell Sullivan

This title represents the first publicly published, not in sequence but in terms of order for reading reference, in a trio of mathematical based books.

The three titles are:

A Question of Intelligence   written first
Mind You P's and Q's   written second
The Book of Things   written third

It is my intention to eventually publish all three. In addition to this, *Going It Alone* may be located at Balboa Press or Amazon.

The Book of Things

Russell Sullivan

To order additional copies of this book, contact:
Xlibris
1-800-455-039
www.Xlibris.com.au
Orders@Xlibris.com.au
725535

CONTENTS

FIGURES

ACKNOWLEDGEMENTS

It was zen and the art of motorcycle maintenance that put a feast on my plate enabling questions, not nonsensical, to formulate clearly for me. My hope is that this addition to the literary table will assist someone else in developing their lexicon.

Everything is a thing, even nothing.

INTRODUCTION

This is a book based upon an extrapolation of some principles taught in mid secondary school science with a notable exception. It is non-science.

Actually it is nonsense.

The issue is how is this nonsense even though it is based around a simple piece of science usable?

There are three aspects to this nonsense required to make it 'work'. Science works[1] which is why it is science, non-science, or nonsense obviously differs.

So does this make nonsense of nonsense?

No.

Nonsense is constructed using three basic principles.

These three principles are:

First, *conjecture*. This is not verifiable like science. This lowly form of logic is the cornerstone of nonsense, or non-science. While science may be the key to our present and our future, nonsense has a value. It is just that, unlike science, nonsense is considered far less valuable as a commodity or building block.

Second, *correctional factors*. Plus or minus by absolute values or percentages, these are used to adjust non-science calculations to the point of, at least, sense, albeit nonsense.

---

[1] 'Aesthetics aside, the ultimate test of a physical theory is its ability to explain and predict phenomena accurately' (Greene, B, *The Elegant Universe* (Vintage, London, 2005), p. 76).

Third, *immeasurables*. Science has bashed down the frontiers of so many things. Immeasurables differ in that they cannot (and most likely will not) be verified or quantified to a level that science advocates it will eventually attain.

Armed with these three tools, nonsense, or non-science, can be developed. Using some very simple science as its basis, non-science will be developed within these pages.

A simple illustration to distinguish between the basis of nonsense, or non-science, in comparison to science is to show two different views of the same thing, with each view slightly different to illustrate the contextual understanding and basis of both non-science and science.

Figure 1: Questionable science.   Figure 2: More questionable science.

The images in figures 1 and 2 represent a view of science, or scientific enquiry. They are abstract, multifaceted and ponderable.

This is science and modern science, which confounds with paradoxes and dimensional views that render the absurd inane and the inane interesting. It is an interesting counterpoint to science and scientific enquiry of ages gone by.

Applied science is, of course, how science—through scientific method and the application of both simple and abstract modes of thought, such as those depicted in figures 1 and 2—are made applicable to everyday existence. Scientific method and proof are intrinsic to the notion of applied science, and it is the application of science that provides further evidence and lowers barriers to refutation.

Figure 3: A non-scientific view.

What then is non-science?

Figure 3 is simple, non-abstract, and potentially unable to be applied. Unlike science, non-science does not require verification, nor does it claim potential application.

Let us consider a specific example. Water is a liquid, and when frozen, it becomes ice. The thawed ice returns to water again. Heat, though, may be applied, and that water will become a gas.

All these changes require some degree of energy and result in a different arrangement of the molecules in which the original water (molecularly H_2O) is arranged.

Each of these various arrangements of the molecular structure of in this example water in non-science, or this nonsensical non-scientific view, shall be termed states. The actual means by which the alteration of states occurs and other such factors will be given occasional regard. However, they are the basis of science, and non-science need not consider them

This book of non-science then considers states and the different states of matter. The science that (like heating and thawing) provides the interactions between these states is what science has considered and proven over many years.

Welcome to non-science.

It is possible readers will come to the conclusion that this book does not add up. That is potentially correct, and any mathematical ideas are expressed for the sake of discussion and to enable a book that did not add up, mind your *Ps* and *Qs* to add up. The only question for the reader at the end of this book is whether or not non-science is nonsense.

A final note to the reader is that *The Book of Things* is so dated in its approach potentially to those who deal with quantum that it is

Euclidean. Euclid, of course, is one whose mathematical achievements the writer aspires. This is not to denigrate the great man or associate him with nonsense.

The X Factor

To enable a clearer distinction than non-sense and potentially the application of actual formal analysis (should it be desired), then an X factor has been considered the simplest basis.

The X factor is simply applied as a substitution for each of the different fields of study or enquiry covered within this book. An example is astrophysics which is an existing and universally accepted field of study.

Substituting the first character of that particular field with X results in *Xstrophysics*. Those wishing to consider any of the other disciplines mentioned or implied within these pages as a field of enquiry may choose to adopt the X factor to distinguish it from the existing and accepted field.

How to Read This Book

It may seem an unusual guideline, a how-to-read-a-book guide; however the sciences are full of tables, formulae, methodologies, and other means by which those who are to follow or utilise the knowledge gained and later applied as science are required to understand.

Why should non-science be different? Nonsense does not need instruction; however, this book of nonsense is constructed using a combination of methods.

To hopefully provide greater pleasure for the reader and a better understanding of how the notions of conjecture, correctional factors, and immeasurables may be applied, this section will provide some guidelines.

In the first instance, this book includes some illustration. These images are designed, in part, to assist with better enabling the comprehension of the subject matter, but they are also for the author to display artistic endeavour.

An example follows, and the character to be introduced in figure 4 has the unusual name of Ert.

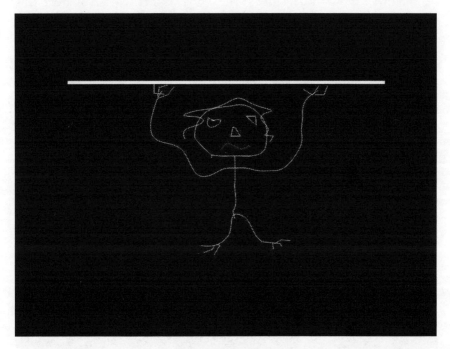

Figure 4: Meet Ert.

Ert is named after his home planet, Ertia. Those who visit there are provided with the tourist guide to being in Ertia, a pun on a dialect pronunciation that those from Ertia encountered on a faraway planet.

Ert is standing beneath a line. What is the significance of this? The line is one-dimensional, and those who have had social encounters with Ert may also consider him to be somewhat one-dimensional as an Ertian. Interesting how the characterisation of those from one planet to another somehow manages to find criticism.

Ert, though is about to do something interesting. Ert is going to take hold of that one-dimensional line and, through the simple process of applying downward pressure, change it.

The question is whether or not Ert or other Ertians for that matter are also perhaps able to expand or alter what some may see as a somewhat basic personality in a similar way.

Figure 5 shows the results of the efforts of Ert. Unfortunately, this book is unable to similarly illustrate any changes in the one-dimensional personality of Ert.

Figure 5: Ert, two-dimensionally framed.

To finalise this section of the how-to guide, Ert will rotate this two-dimensional shape slightly. What do you think will happen?

Figure 6 reveals the results.

Figure 6: Ert in a three-dimensional world.

Ert now inhabits a three-dimensional space.

This rudimentary use of illustration will be found throughout these pages. Occasionally, as an artist may use a broad canvas to better portray a subject the illustrations will be in landscape or sideways. This is to provide dramatic effect and has been borrowed as a tool from those who so faithfully ply their wares in the art world.

Like Ert, those who encounter these images will be required to undertake the simple exercise of rotating the page sideways to view the image more fully.

A Little Bit of Nonsense

How then, if science is to be applied to justify its own ends, can non-science be applied? Of course, it is nonsense; however, sometimes even trying to comprehend the foolish has some benefit, and so the following is a little bit of nonsense.

Let us commence with our third item for inclusion in non-science.

Immeasurability

Things may be immeasurable for many reasons. The example that has been selected relates to our first palette. A scaled-down illustration is provided in figure 7.

Figure 7: A dark space.

Figure 7 is a rectangle, and rectangles may be analysed and measured in many ways. One measurement is the area:

$$\text{area } (A) = \text{length } (L) \times \text{width } (W)$$

This type of formula may be used for different shapes, such as a circle. The formula for the area of a circle is:

$$* A = \pi r^2$$

The subject of this example may simply be symbolically represented as ∞.

This particular symbol has been chosen as it represents infinity. Infinity is, of course, immeasurable, although interestingly some may say that this is not the case.

Let us introduce our first element for non-science—conjecture.

Con. 1: That infinity may be no larger than the minuscule, everything that exists being portrayed and existing in a form of prismatic jigsaw.

This of course is a statement for the point of illustration, not an item of conjecture for this particular book. Note that the conjecture has been given an identifier (Con.) and the example number (1).

Unlike this notion of conjecture infinity is infinite. The fact that it can be reduced to a small symbol illustrates both the ability and need for even immeasurables, such as infinity, to be represented.

Our first artistic representation follows.

Workspaces

The palette represents a workspace.

Workspaces are like the palette covered in oil paints that daub on to an easel. Non-science and this book use the idea of workspaces to assist in defining subjects.

The first step in using a workspace, like the artist's easel, is to create a workspace. The artist needs an easel and the non-scientist in this instance has chosen a drawing.

Our first workspace may be measured as it is a rectangle, the measurement of interest for this workspace being its area. Of further interest in our workspace are the identifiers. Each workspace has two identifying characteristics that are included at the upper right-hand corner. These are:

1. Workspace identifier (WID): In this instance, the workspace is infinity. This has been abbreviated to the first two characters of the word and has three dots (...) below to indicate that it is a workspace.
2. Temporal identifier (TID): The temporal identifier, or time identifier, is a means of identifying when in time an event or workspace has been depicted. The identifier commences with a t followed by a decimal number between minus one (-1) and one (1).

The decimal identifier may be incremented by small values and, to increase or decrease the scale of accuracy, raised to a power n times.

In addition to the inclusion of these identifiers, the TID may be followed by the following symbols:

a: arbitrary
e: estimated

i: irrelevant (replaces numeric notation)
u: unknown (replaces numeric notation)

Let us then further analyse this nonsensical view of infinity using the second criterion for non-science correctional factors.

Having created a workspace that is infinite, it (like the artist and the easel) it is now possible to work in an infinite area. The area is of course not infinite. It is notionally infinite, with the (...) notation representing notional.

"Eureka" some may say, "we are now able to work on an infinite workspace." The area of this workspace is calculated as ∞.

Of course, there is a fly in the ointment, being that our workspace is portrayed in this instance as a rectangle.

If for instance a person were to work on a workspace that was a piece of paper measuring 10 centimetres long by 5 centimetres wide, it would have an area of 50 centimetres ($A = L \times W$).

Our notional workspace actually is incorrect by the area it is contained within; hence, it is ∞ minus 50 centimetres.

Now, it measures a correctly infinite value.

Our illustration of non-science is complete. The three components immeasurability, conjecture, and correctional factors are utilised in the creation of a workspace.

Is this nonsense? That is for the reader to ascertain as subjectivity permeates all ideas and non-science is no different to science in that regard.

Life's Little Luxuries

Do you eat chocolate?
Caviar?
Drink champagne?
Drive a high performance motor vehicle?

These are luxuries or considered luxuries in the broader social context. Some people can afford different levels of luxury to others, and in a strange twist of fate, non-science has a luxury unavailable to its scientific counterpart.

Motive or motivation.

Science and indeed modern society are driven by incentive. Money being one; however, there are many others. Non-science differs in that in the overall societal context, it has no necessarily determinable result.

What then will motivate any form of enquiry into non-science? This is a dilemma, and the dilemmas that confront those who may be interested in non-science are discussed more fully before any person should consider continuing with any form of enquiry into the nonsense (that is, non-science).

The Resultant Dilemma

The resultant dilemma is a malady, or affliction, that many in various fields of endeavour throughout history (however, possibly more so in modern society) suffer from.

What is the resultant dilemma?

It can be defined as the need, driven by either internal or external motivating factors or motivators, or the produced results and the dilemma faced by those seeking to attain such results when those results are not attained.

Pressure cooker roles of employees, the scientist whose laboratory requires funding, or perhaps the artisan struggling for that elusive creative spark—the resultant dilemma in these and many other instances can be ruinous.

Industry, society, and even individuals fuel the fires of these pressure cooker ovens. Money requires results, and while there are still altruistic endeavours in society, they are not the norm. In some instances that an individual whose hobby or labour of love their passion in life can in itself drive a form of individual pressure cooker, rather than the external motivator, such as the financier, the individual berate and chastise themselves.

Self-flagellation as seen in some of television's more gruesome tales, is replaced by a different form of torment—failure or disappointment.

Society though seems to have found the 'norm' of the motivator and considers it a necessary evil. What then of those items not considered worth either individual or societal investment?

These do not suffer from the resultant dilemma; rather they are consigned to the wastebasket, those who champion or give rise to such ideas, watching them wither compared to their more desirous counterparts.

Perhaps a short story will illustrate such a point:

> Once upon a time, in a deep dark forest, inaccessible to the world without, lived a creature—a heinous, gruesome beast capable of even driving away the wolves that prowled this dark domain.
>
> Not the great lion, ravenous bear, but an avian. A bird.
>
> This was a wild goose.

Figure 8: The wild goose.

The goose, of course, has been domesticated to the extent that a goose can be domesticated in those more accessible reaches of the globe where humanity has set foot.

Humanity, however, has not found its way into the dark domain. High mountain plateaus and impenetrable vine forests have prevented all, with the exception of the hardiest creatures, from making such a journey.

One of which was the goose.

How it was that the goose and indeed geese, as there are families that inhabit the dark domain, made their way is not to be found as an historical record. The wild goose, unfortunately, did not mark cave walls or scribe the history of its passing as humanity does.

So it can only be surmised that, at some point, a family on route via the air were thrust into this wilderness by some turbulence.

Stories of the wild goose flew far and wide.

Fables.

The yeti of the Himalayas, Sasquatch (or Bigfoot) of the Americas, and Yowie of Terra Australis are also fabled creatures that have attracted the attention of many an expedition and adventurer.

Photographic evidence, documentaries, and theories abound as to these creatures and their habits. And so it was that—'the wild goose chase' was undertaken.

A wild goose chase?

So named as it was seeking that wild goose.

Expeditions set forth with maps and compasses. Charts were made of territories hitherto unknown and unexplored to ascertain the whereabouts not only of the wild goose but also its mysterious hidden domain.

The expeditioners, understanding the ferocity of what they sought, were well prepared with many an apparatus of self-protection.

So the stories spread, and as each expedition returned—as was the case with those other fabled creatures, including the yeti—the wild goose chase gathered a momentum of its own.

Success though was not for the taking. Failure beset each expedition until eventually the wild goose chase was considered to be just that—a wild goose chase.

And as failure comes at a price, this quest for the wild goose was considered the domain of the foolhardy, and the resultant dilemma was that no one bothered to chase that wild goose.

Other mythical creatures suffered the same fate, being considered the domain of the foolish, yet the wild goose and indeed wild goose chase had achieved a unique notoriety.

So many other forms of foolish endeavour were so named the wild goose chase.

For those interested in gaining sponsorship or requiring results, the wild goose chase is likely to arrive at the resultant dilemma.

So do wild goose chases still occur? Does society have a place for such, or does that motivator to produce results still drive all?

And what of that wild goose? It still abounds in its hidden domain, doubtless to be the subject of future quests and speculation.

The Ethical Dilemma

The ethical dilemma is a quandary.

Ethics itself is a quandary, and the ethical dilemma has been posed to science in a multitude of forms and on a multitude of occasions.

Simplistically, the ethical dilemma is the question of whether to act or not to act. Science, as per the discussion regarding the resultant dilemma, produces outcomes.

Results.

These results then drive actions.

A result of these actions, using simple cause-and-effect analysis, is change. Change can create benefit; however, it can also create instability and even uncertainty.

Those luxuries of chocolates, caviar, champagne, and the high-performance vehicle were outcomes from human endeavour. They are what people savour, and as they are what people savour, there will be a demand for them.

Economics is built on this simple notion, and as society has progressed, then people's desires have been sated further and further, and those who indulge in science fiction as distinct from science or non-science will assume that change will continue to be promulgated and our desires sated further into the future.

Nirvana.

Utopia.

Idealism and idealists.

Is this then not beneficial? Karl Marx, an economist of a different ilk, may not necessarily have agreed with the simplistic utopian mechanism that is demand-driven. He developed a different but more controlled social ideal. It would seem than that like philosophy this somehow is intrinsic to the development of society as a whole.

What then of non-science? A simple story illustrates the perspective from the non-scientific change provocateur.

> Sitting atop a mountain peak, surrounded by verdant lands, a rock considered relocation. Years had passed in which the rock had cast its eye at the vista of a distant peak.
>
> Would the grass be greener on the other side?
> Philosophically speaking should the rock relocate?

This is a question of upheaval, of migration not by a creature such as the caribou but an entity nonetheless.

The upheaval was more literally being in the physics of a rock actually lifting its weight and creating the momentum to move to that distant spot. It is conjecture; however, this author considers that science of course would say the rock was moved by nature, perhaps a landslide, and that the upheaval was of little consequence as in this remote location it did not affect higher-level sentient creatures.

The issue then for the higher level sentient creature is, should they change? Embrace upheaval and continue to embrace upheaval as the benefits of those luxuries and continued benefits espoused in literature, such as science fiction, would attest.

Non-science has no apparent benefits or social context. The rock cannot think, it is an analogous statement belonging to literature and some may say nonsense. Hence, it managed to contextually and neatly find a place within these pages.

The ethical dilemma that results from questions regarding science and science fiction regarding change, progression, and upheaval to provide that social benefit contextually belongs more to that rock than society in general.

Non-science simply sits and ponders, requiring external stimuli, such as that landslide, to provide any change or motivation. The conundrum for those interested in non-science, then, is like that rock. Why bother?

Lessons Learned

This completes the introductory and explanatory section of *The Book of Things*. It may seem nonsense to some that a book would include instructions; however non-science is considered to in some way resemble its counterpart. Science requires at least a modicum of structure.

There are of course many fields of mathematics and science and non-science borrows heavily from them. In addition to this it has pilfered the artisan's tools to render canvas and imagery that hopefully assist those who may have chanced upon these pages.

Having introduced the elements of expression and the artisan's pallet we will proceed and explain the basic tenets of states. Why the idea of using states as a basis of explaining ideas was chosen will only become apparent as these pages unfold.

Of course it can result in those who may read these pages declaring them nonsense.

OPENING STATEMENTS

Let us first consider a question as the methodology for progressing towards this analysis of states. The question mark was introduced as the diagrammatic delineation between science and non-science, and this delineation shall remain fundamental to the analysis prepared in these pages.

The question that can be asked regarding an analysis of the states of matter is "Does this matter?" Modern science (and for the purposes of temporal notation this is the year 2012) has the ability to scrutinise matter using microscopes, particle accelerators, and myriad other instruments.

This is non-science and a notable differentiation between non-science and science is that non-science is not reliant upon instrumentation. The faculties that provide and produce logic are not defined as instruments by non-science enabling their application.

This does not mean that non-science cannot use instrumentation, and indeed the basis for much of the logic included within these pages uses information gleaned from scientific apparatus to provide some elements of substantiation to the discussions. However logic remains the primary tool given the three elements that have been outlined as the basis for non-scientific argument.

The following section introduces the basic ideas that underpin this analysis of matter and the states in which matter, using scientific instrumentation, has been ascertained to be arranged. A non-scientific notation at the commencement is an item of conjecture:

> Con. 1: The arrangements of matter depicted within this section are broad enough to encapsulate what science would describe at this point in time.

With our first item of conjecture, a simple logical statement, the exploration of matter, begins.

The Basics

Prior to discussing matters of state, it is usual to make some deliberation as to how such matters should be addressed. This is something of a play on words, of course, just like the usage of science and non-science that underpins these pages is playfully transposed to nonsense. Matters of state are of course serious issues that are attributed to governments or institutions of importance.

As science and non-science are carefully delineated in these pages, the possible playful coining of matters of state, which is the core topic of this book, has now (to some extent) been delineated.

How then should the matter regarding states be considered without scientific apparatus?

Fortunately, an entity named Ert found himself stranded upon an alien planet known as Earth by those who are its indigenous inhabitants. Ert, of course, has a history of being in the wrong place at the wrong time. How else can the fact that he strayed from his home planet to another be commented upon? And it is with the assistance of Ert that the matter of state shall initially be reviewed.

Ertians, like humans, require sustenance and Ert has momentarily paused for a drink of cold water. Those who observe figure 9 closely may notice that the water has ice cubes in it. These are of course different to the liquid in which they float and require Ert to either suck or chew in order to consume them.

Figure 9: Ert and the solid state.

They are solid. If you were to look more closely, the strange orange bubbles in the ice are molecules. Magnified to be visible, they are quite closely packed.

As Ert moves away from his drink, you may notice that his habit of being in that wrong place has resulted in a collision with a wall. The wall of course is solid, and so it is with the assistance of Ert (although he is nursing a sore head after bumping into that wall) that the first state, or *solids*, can be ascertained.

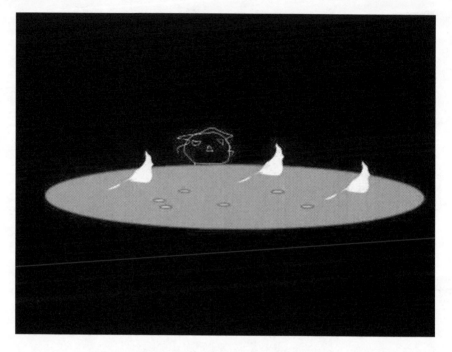

Figure 10: Ert suffering from liquidity problems.

Ert, of course, manages to lurch from one issue to another and so it is that suddenly, after rebounding off a wall and moving outside a further dilemma presents itself.

Those familiar with finance may have some knowledge of what constitutes a liquidity problem. Of course Ert is not in financial trouble as the Ertian currency unit, or Erg, is not acceptable on Earth.

Ert has fallen into the sea.

The substance surrounding Ert—not the fins belonging to a perilous ocean predator but the blue substance unlike that wall—allowed Ert to penetrate below the surface quite easily.

A close look may indicate that there are bubbles akin to those within the ice cubes however these are more widely spread. This structure is liquid and hopefully Ert is able to swim.

Our second state is a *liquid*.

Amazingly Ert has managed to extract himself from the liquid peril and now is resting upon a remote island. This may sound idyllic conjuring up images of exotic fruits, but it is not the case. Unfortunately Ert has landed upon a volcanic island.

Figure 11 depicts this unusual scene.

Figure 11: Ert's gastronomical adventure.

The island is located in a warm part of the globe and while this may be uncomfortable for a person, Ert has encountered a further dilemma.

He took a brief swim to bathe after his recent salty episode. The water warms and the air is full of steam. Beneath the island, lava has suddenly crept its way upwards and now is heating the land. This heat combined with the water creates a gas, steam.

Our third state is *gas* or a *gaseous state*.

At this juncture non-science or nonsense, and nonsensical ideas like a gas permeate these pages. In order to progress a palette will be used.

Our first palette was somewhat rudimentary and depicted infinity. Infinity denoted with the identifier *In* or symbol ∞. The use of three full stops (…) below the symbolic notation creates our workspace.

Those familiar with the science of chemistry will perhaps know how elements are described—example: water being H (hydrogen) and O (oxygen). A table of non-scientific symbols is included as an appendix in this book.

Science provided the first three states; however, non-science shall progress beyond this definition using a very simple palette. The palette has the identifier Mo (molecular) and uses a very familiar symbol as its core image.

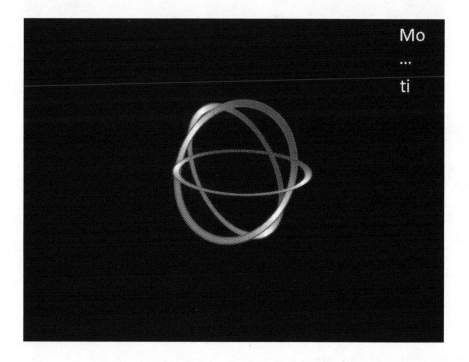

Ert has been found and travelled back to his home location on Earth. Going out for his evening walk, he has made the mistake of stubbing his toe on the ground.

"Ouch" Ert exclaims as many people or Ertians would.

Figure 12: Ert's trans missions.

The *fourth* state is what can collectively be described as transmissions.

The molecular structure of what constitutes a transmission differs from the composition of elements such as water described in the first three states.

Ert having kicked his toe and exclaimed has called for help. This message was being relayed as a sound to a person who was located some distance away—750 miles away. The speed of sound is 750 miles per hour and sound is transmitted, such as the words from Ert as a wave. Of course science fiction and later science have intimated that the notion of the molecular nature outlined as the first three states may be transmissible.

Teleportation or the transmission of matter through space alters the state in which matter exists, like water being converted to ice. However unlike being converted from one of the first three states, it is altered to being more akin to the fourth state.

This allows molecules, such as water, to be transmitted at speeds such as the speed of light (670 million miles per hour, or 186,000 miles per second) rather than the speed of sound. If only Ert could have teleported rather than yelled his call for help.

Figure 12 is full of waves in rainbow-like colours. A simple way of observing light is through a prism or a looking glass.

There are many other forms of transmissions though including gamma rays or delta rays, each of these being measured by various scientific devices. While Ert has been a useful assistant for non-scientific analysis and measurement it is at levels such as these that modern science has progressed and non-science utilises the science gained from its formal counterpart.

Ert, though has been involved in one final encounter. It was with something so infinitesimally small that he was unable to see it.

A bullet travels at a speed that renders it invisible to the eye.

Ert has encountered something that travels at a speed more closely associated with the speed of light, a particle. Items in the fifth state are called *particles*.

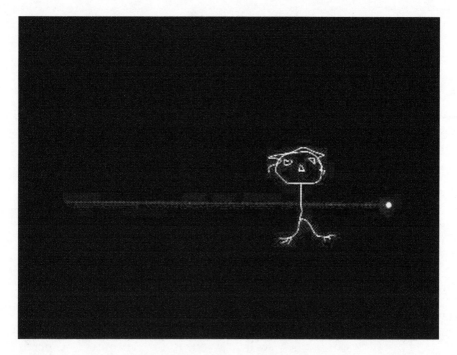

Figure 13: Ert being very particular.

The photon is a particle of light and travels at the speed of light. There are many other particles, including neutrinos and quarks.

The change in the workspace from the infinite to molecular enables the notion of viewing larger states of matter, such as solids or gases which are macroscopic or visible when aggregated to microscopic or invisible items.

Workspaces then alter the landscape from the perspective of the reader between conceptual notions such as these, and it is for this reason, in addition to an element of artistic largesse, that they have been included.

In Addition To

The subject matter until this point has and (for the majority of this book) will remain the notion of states. However, as a token gesture and for the sake of completeness, the addition of some additional elements will be included.

Our initial discussion regarding states mentioned the simple processes of heating and cooling altering the state of water. This was expanded to extend beyond water and consider other types of matter.

Those familiar with physics may scoff at these ideas, or perhaps others may have (like the author) a basic understanding of physics and the universe gleaned from the works of others. To provide some completeness to that view of the universe and combine matters a brief discussion of the greater universe follows.

Rather than states, each of the elements mentioned will be grouped together as *forces.*

Forces have intrinsic characteristics—not the least of which is that they affect or alter other items with which they have contact. Here is a list of the items that, in summary, are considered to encapsulate the forces that underpin the cosmological clock that is the universe:

1. gravity
2. magnetism

3. collisions
4. erosion
5. volcanism
6. tectonics.

Like heating and cooling affected the water molecule, these forces affect the universe as a whole. The addition of these items to our listing of basic states until this point is considered relevant to this book in providing completeness to the idea of the universe as a working totality that encapsulates those basic states discussed thus far.

Summing Up

This concludes the outline of the basic states and a rudimentary summation of the cosmos from a non-science perspective.

Is it nonsense? Possibly.

ABOUT THINGS

It is time to move further from the realms of science towards the basis of non-science.

While the initial aspects of this book may not necessarily correlate directly with scientific views in 2012, they cannot be considered to deviate so drastically to completely deserve the label of nonsense.

In addition to this, a book concerning states that is titled *The Book of Things* is also somewhat anomalous. What then is the significance of things?

First a quote from a little known text:

> Things: Any physical or intangible item, real or imaginary, and able to be perceived by the naked eye or not.[2]

The definition is of little consequence to many people as it has been derived from a book that perhaps was more nonsensical than this, yet it was necessary for the completion of this work. Why quote from such a little-known text? Self-aggrandisement perhaps as it is the same author?

---

[2] R. J. Sullivan, *A Question of Intelligence: Update for Reappraisal* (PAUONH Books: Victoria, 2012), 34.

No.

Context.

A reference to another text enables a single statement to be given a contextual place in an overall body of work. This is analogously the simplest manner to explain the notion of things in a comprehensible way.

Words belong in sentences, sentences in paragraphs, paragraphs in chapters and chapters in books. To minimise the need to write or paraphrase entire sections of work the simple referencing of one idea transfers the contextual meaning.

If you think then of words as things and those sentences, paragraphs, chapters and books not as pages but as space, then things exist in space.

The words stated by Ert were conveyed across space to that other person. Words then exist as they are transmissible and transmitted.

Not only words, but all ideas and events exist as things in space using this simple analogous method. What then are the states in which those things exist?

The original thought on this issue was to discuss super states—that is, to separate the original intent of the book from a desire to discuss how certain specific ideas or systems exist as things in massive coordinated patterns.

Like molecules' their arrangement distinguishes their specific traits and identifies them, these arrangements are themselves unique and separately distinguishable.

However the designation of these items as things homogenises the characteristic of matter enabling them to be discussed as states and maintaining continuity throughout this book.

Each of these states though, due to their complexity shall be introduced via a workspace, enabling artistic expression and establishing that conceptual super state even though the original idea was discarded.

These states are:

1. the temporal state
2. the financial state
3. the digital state
4. the quantum state
5. the natural state
6. the emotional state
7. the realistic state
8. the state.

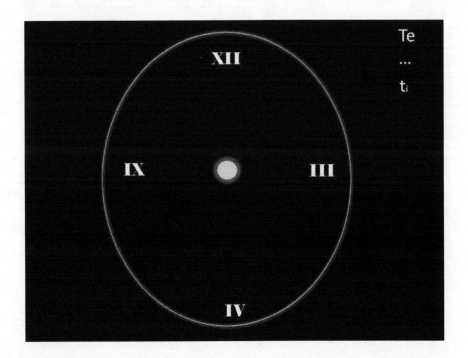

The Temporal State

What would you do if you had all the time in the world?

There are many answers to this question. It can be answered literally—and the issue of physically housing a significant number of timepieces considered—perhaps in terms of life's journey and a slow travail across wilderness and society with occasional companions given.

This is time.

Multi-faceted.

Time has as many faces as a clock has minutes.

At this point a person may try to give themselves some latitude; this linguistically is possible but not temporally.

The sundial and study of the heavens in early history provided an amazing array of calendars to record seasons and history. Observing the movements above the Earth provided a means to measure how it was behaving better than by observing the planet alone could provide.

Those first timepieces were carved in stone precursors to their latter-day descendants intricately constructed from woodwork and eventually metals.

It was the need again to measure the Earth that forced time and the study of time to progress along these lines. Longitude needed some latitude and while instruments such as the eyeglass and sextant could ascertain the latter, the former was as elusive as a black cat on a darkened evening.

Metals in the form of heavy metals and isotopic decay rates were then deviously measured to calculate time to even more fathomable accurate terms.

Time is sometimes depicted or discussed as a dimension, and space-time is differentiated from its earthly counterpart. Time is eternal and time is decadent thumbing its nose at the finite limitations imposed upon those who dwell within its walls.

Interestingly though, humanity—after learning to measure time—decided to manipulate time.

Recording, prerecording, and re-recording all these elements that came after the progression from astral observation to other forms of observation as records of events enabled time to be manipulated as never before.

Humanity was the master of time. The beast in its lair had been championed. How can this be achieved?

Simple and rudimentary mathematics. The illustration of the timescales provided within the scaling factors section is applied as pluses and minuses enabling events to be after, then before, then after, then before.

Time is the sixth state and time now belongs to us.

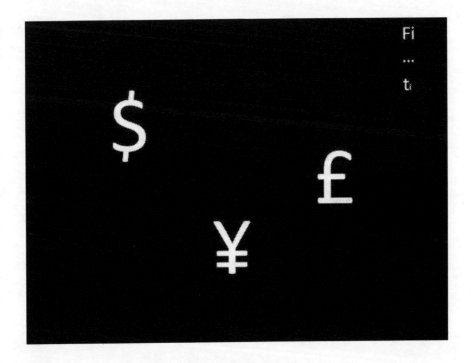

The Financial State

They say money makes the world go round.

This then qualifies all things financial for inclusion as physical bodies, one would think.

Those age-old theories of astral rotation at the whim of a larger mass in space termed the Sun were debunked by modern science.

That non-science was replaced by a new thinking.

Early humanity gathered from the land and had no need nor care for the modern paradigm of financial exchange. To best illustrate the marvels of finance, rather than turn to history, a short piece of legal terminology is a useful analogy.

> A bill of exchange is an unconditional order in writing, addressed by one person to another, signed by the person giving it, requiring the person to whom it is addressed to pay on demand, or at a fixed or determinable future time, a sum certain in money to or to the order of a specified person, or to bearer.
>
> (2) An instrument which does not comply with these conditions, or which orders any act to be done in addition to the payment of money, is not a bill of exchange.
>
> (3) An order to pay out of a particular fund is not unconditional within the meaning of this section; but an unqualified order to pay, coupled with:
>
> (a) an indication of a particular fund out of which the drawee is to re-imburse himself or herself, or a particular account to be debited with the amount; or

(b) a statement of the transaction which gives rise to the bill;

is unconditional.

(4) A bill is not invalid by reason:

(a) that it is not dated;

(b) that it does not specify the value given, or that any value has been given therefor; or

(c) that it does not specify the place where it is drawn, or the place where it is payable. [3]

This section of text illustrates where finance has progressed beyond money. It is as complex as the structure of atoms and intrinsic to the operations of the financial system.

Finance has even developed its own mathematical language. An example is the money multiplier expressed as:

$$m = \frac{MoneyStock}{MonetaryBase} = \frac{Deposits + PubliclyHeldCurrency}{MonetaryBase} = \frac{1+\gamma}{\alpha + \beta + \gamma}$$

This provides some basic insight into the financial state, perhaps a little history. Cowries were early examples of what became known as currency progressing beyond exchange of goods known as barter. Gold and rare or precious items then filled the social void needed to enable trade.

Money was agreed and the United States was something of a pioneer in the progression from a resource-based tradable commodity to cash.

---

[3] Bills of Exchange Act 1909, section 8, Australian government.

It may be that as society progresses cash will diminish, and electronic money will enable even greater levels of trade and availability.

This is the *financial* state.

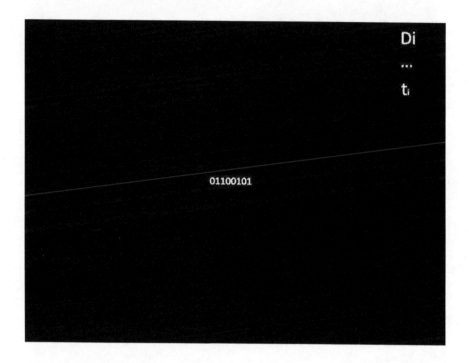

The Digital State

If there was ever a Frankenstein, is it the digital state?

Created by man this child was born of the fluxes of energy and rendered in zeros and ones to create almost anything imaginable.

The digital state is both finite and infinite.

Virtually no bounds are known and the limitations of the physical universe rendered using those ones and zeroes are a feeble comparison.

Modern society languishes yet lavishes itself luxuriously with digitisation from early harmonic resonances to the unknown future where perhaps humanity itself, according to some, may find existence in the digital state preferable to their natural state.

Those interested in numerical and decimal-notated events may investigate the Turing machine and universal Turing machine. These devices and mathematical concepts regard the infinite as a series of steps and are universal in their application to the laws of physics.

Computing developed from the embryo as punched card systems, and in less than a single human generation it leapt into the realms of processing units. These machines rapidly replaced early technology and computers, and computing eye the quantum world with envy.

Communications intermingle with the processing capacity, while data and data storage were reduced from warehouses to thimbles. Satellites and the Internet paved the way for global interaction, with the latest cloud computing technology further defining the modern communication era.

The digital state is transient though. Solar flares are often regarded as a potential culprit for the ruination of the digital age.

> Transience is akin to mortality and while some may regard the modern phenomena of digitising the mind and memory as some potential way of using the digital state to sidestep the limitations of human existence, the digital state is in itself finite.

This is transience, and while it is a temporary panacea for the age-old human lurgies that result in the demise of the self, in some areas, it is perhaps regarded as some form of digital salvation. This is the power that the digital state in some areas has over the imagination. Virtual reality and social escapism define the new computing revolution, and the digital state is being further and further embedded into everyday existence.

The digital state and media integration further entrench the social importance of the digital state and its place as a social norm. The question—like the question of evolution to some and those question marks that differentiated science and non-science—is where the digital state will progress to and what its eventual role in society shall become.

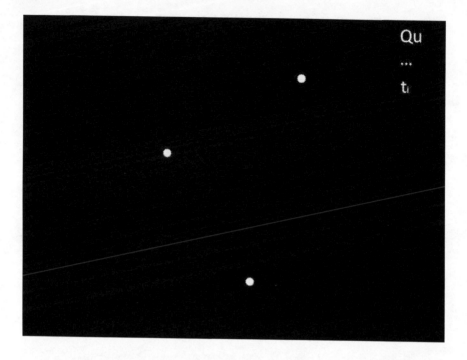

The Quantum State

Quantum and the quantum world are relative newcomers to this listing. A world so strange it is considered by some as being inexplicable. Some things are best left to explain to those specialised in the area, so let us quote from the world of physics:

> Nevertheless the debate about quantum mechanics really continues unabated. Everyone agrees on how to use the equations of quantum theory to make predictions. But there is no consensus on what it really means to have probability waves, nor how a particle chooses which of its own possible futures to follow, nor even on whether it really does choose or instead splits off like a branching tributary to live out all possible futures in an ever-expanding arena of parallel universes. These

interpretational issues are worthy of a book-length discussion in their own right.[4]

For that reason, the exploration and explanation of the *quantum* state shall not progress beyond this point.

The Natural State

Mother Nature sat on her own with crayons and proceeded to draw a landscape.

Being female she rendered more subtle nuances and spurned the charcoals of Father Nature for a rainbow-based palette, butterflies, and laughing children.

---

[4]   B. Greene, *The Elegant Universe* (Vintage, 2005), 108.

Those who (like Father Nature) are somewhat particular may have noticed that the abbreviated name for nature was Nt and not Na. This is to prevent an overlap with the naming conventions used in chemistry Na with this abbreviation.

Of course some say convention should be applied and adhered to so should such a criticism be lodged, then it is duly noted by the author.

The natural state has so many images that the idea of biodiversity expressed as a way of encapsulating what is only a fragment of the natural state can be utilised as nature diversity.

From the allure of the physique to the manure of the pit, the natural state appeals and appals. It is easy to fall into the trap of surveying your surroundings and expressing awe at the sheer audacity Mother Nature had in devising something so intricate.

The natural state can be considered all-encompassing, yet it exists in its own right and is better represented as an entity in itself.

Of course the natural state and the laws of nature have been studied and documented. Nature has its own laws and these provide some insights into how this entity came to be.

There is a profundity of literature to describe the natural state, and it has inspired music, art, and many other forms of flattery and mimicry.

It is hoped, or intended that the discussions regarding states will become more natural as time goes by.

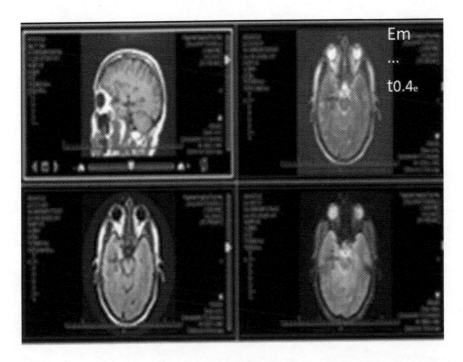

The Emotional State

Welcome to the neuroverse.

The emotional state is so termed due to its very foundation comprising a grid so complex it exceeds the complexity of society itself even in the twenty-first century, powered by an energy source capable of travelling at the speed of light or even faster.

The brain is the factory that energises the emotional state. It is a profundity mixed with integrated circuitry to rival the digital state composed of neurons. Electrical charges travel between these neurons creating a physical state that is measurable as a state of physics.

Modern magnetic imaging technology has enabled this internal circuitry to be exposed and viewed as never before. The neuroverse is more than simple neurons. Chemicals and hormones abound, and stimuli from the human host or entity that the emotional state interacts with transmit signals that provide information regarding that aspect of the natural state.

The emotional state is complex, unstable, rational, irrational, and prone to error. It also is the labyrinth where emotions of elation and depression, intermingled with envy, pleasure, desire, anger, or joy, are just some of the myriad examples.

How the neuroverse and the universe interact has and remains a topic of much interest and speculation. Notions of consciousness, awareness, and transcendence are only some of the areas that the human condition has attempted to be reconciled with some greater universal or cosmic state.

It is this interest and almost introspection that perhaps promotes the emotional state as a significant state in comparative terms. That question mark or those question marks defining both science and non-science will have no place at all among the molecular states without the emotional state.

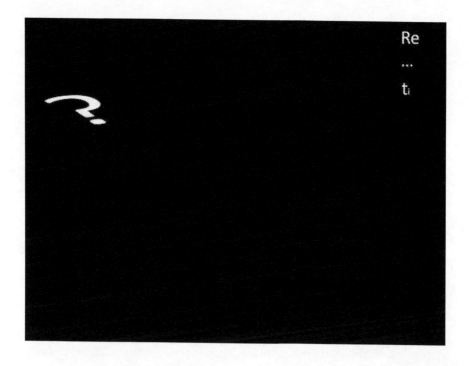

The Realistic State

What is reality?

This may seem a trite question and reality as a state, unrealistic. Reality though via the works of existentialists and philosophers, has been the subject of much conjecture.

The basis of conjecture flows from these fields of thought on to these pages itself.

Reality can be considered in terms of life itself. Why is it that some people progress through life with seeming ease while others struggle to manage?

Why did that motor vehicle travelling so urgently to an airport destination cease its progress so teasingly close yet (due to time once again pressing its influence into the equation of life) inexorably and irrevocably late?

Why did that building collapse at that particular moment just as that person departed and a miraculous escape from the clutches of fate ensue?

Reality, of course, is also considered regarding matters of the cosmos itself. Is the universe:

a. solid
b. liquid
c. gas
d. none of the above
e. something else

In addition to this is the universe folded and wrapped to resemble a pterodactyl? Where is that pterodactyl going and how did it get such a long beak?

This is *reality*.

The State

How can a state be judged a state?

Interestingly enough the ideas of judges and judging are synonymous with what in social terms can be considered the state.

The state, as distinct from the states being considered within these pages, is a form of social order or social structure that has developed and continues to develop.

The state is both an institution and institutions. It is the role of the state to preserve the institution that it itself is and the institutions that it represents. To this extent the state has an importance and a structure.

This structure has developed along different lines both across time and around the world.

Government.

Law.

Education.

Defence.

Finance.

Diplomacy and trade.

These are just some of the myriad roles that define the state. The state is an unusual state, though, in that it is both a macrocosm and microcosm. The many aspects that comprise a society are blended and controlled, albeit with varying degrees of success, by the state.

The state is sentient. Unlike the digital state, the state is dependent not on processors and connections but people and communications. As a sentient being and aggregation of sentient beings, the state struggles to define itself and to control itself. It is a wonder, though, and a testament to what humanity can achieve.

Is There Something Else?

This concludes the discussion regarding things.

Of course there is always something else however, the specific aspect of this book that necessitated or was best expressed using the idea of things is complete.

The issue that was considered regarding super states is still potentially a trap for the unwary. Systems of classification abound, and the utilisation of states is simply a different form of classification.

However this book as a concept does not owe its existence to the classification system of states. It owes its existence to the classification of things which is all-encompassing and hence so easy to utilise.

Everything has its place and this thing, this book has its place among them.

THE FINAL OPUS

It is time to return to the consideration of states at a more minuscule level and specifically relating to nature and natural substances more akin to those that science will consider.

Of course, the non-scientific aspect remains, and nonsense is still a possibility.

A Space Oddity

There are many astral phenomena that can be considered as having structures so unfamiliar to each other that they can be considered as separate states.

This book will consider one specifically as it is fundamental to so much science and as such to non-science. The fourteenth state is a singularity, or black hole. Figure 14 is a depiction of a black hole.

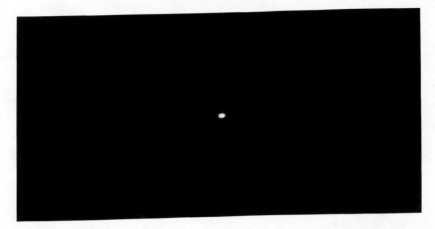

Figure 14: A nano.

Of course this is a rudimentary depiction and lends itself to artistic merit more than scientific representation. What is of interest is that the object is a nano. That being 'one thousand millionth (10^{-9}) the part of'.[5]

Of course, a singularity is not a nano; however, it is time to introduce an element of non-science.

The nano will be corrected by an amount of:

1. minus one thousand millionth to zero as its lower bound
2. a visual acuity factor as its upper bound (this being a degree of increase to enable visibility without the need for microscopic or submicroscopic tools).

The nano now measures a figure that can be represented upon our workspace. Black holes, or singularities, are considered to be objects that, due to the extreme forces that encapsulate them, have a structure of matter that differs significantly enough from those depicted thus far to be termed states.

What else is interesting about this nano is that it has a name—U_1.

Using our palette, U_1 can be viewed as a microscopic object on the background of infinity.

---

5   Gordon and Geddes, *English Dictionary* (Gordon & Geddes: Glasgow, 2010) 287.

Con 2: The universe U_1 is the first universe to contain sentient life; hence, it is so numerically depicted.

The basis for this conjecture is built on several layers. Firstly, the universe U_1 contains a species who miraculously developed language and symbology, eventually enabling them to locate themselves on an astral body, named in the indigenous language of English as Earth.

It is like the inhabitants of that planet who (in its mid history) traversed and intermingled in what can be described as early or first contact. This is due to a variety of factors having many errors in its application.

This universe U_1 derived certain understanding and historical significance from a book known indigenously as the Bible which (like those early explorers) has evidence of the failings of a first contact.

It is possible and has been expressed that there could be several simultaneous universes. This is not the opinion of this book however were it the case and if they were somehow simultaneous or parallel in nature, then their relative positions would render them indistinct, hence numerically equivalent to 1.

There is something of a dilemma with this particular nano. As a depiction of a universe against a backdrop of infinity, it is most probably larger than a nanometre, although perspective and even reality in some schools of thought may challenge such a thing.

Thus, our depiction can be recognised due to the backdrop being infinity, being correct to some sort of scale, as are many maps.

Figure 14 does not depict the workspace notation of either In or ∞ this being due to the desire to create a dual scale notion of the nano and creating the illusion of size with the naming of U_1.

The question then can be asked that if the universe U_1 is not nano-sized and is in fact somewhat larger, then how large is it?

This is difficult to answer, especially as the shape of U_1 itself can only be guessed and as the discussion of the state reality intimated could even perhaps be that of a pterodactyl.

Let us use the non-science model, but prior to that a simple formula. While the area of a rectangle is Length x width as expressed previously, length × width × height provides a three-dimensional area.

Having this simple start point then using non-science, some rudimentary calculations will not necessarily provide an accurate or even near-accurate estimate of the size of U_1 rather they will give some simple illustration of size and hence scale.

> Con 3: For the purposes of estimation in non-science the universe U_1 will be considered not two-dimensional or planar but three-dimensional.

> Con 4: For the purposes of estimation on non-science, a cubic shape rather than cylindrical or other solid object shape shall be assumed.

Having established our rudimentary calculation model using conjecture some correctional factoring is required.

1. In the year 2012 denoted on the planetary body named Earth (henceforth to be noted as E_1) in the universe U_1, the age in E_1-based years of U_1 is 3,700 million based upon estimates provided by some areas of E_1 science.
2. U_1 has been expanding at a rate measured by the scientific basis of red shift over that period.
3. U_1 is not yet middle-aged—that is 0.5 on the linear scale of –1 to 1 used as the non-science measurement gauge. A measure of 0.3 shall be applied.

Let us try a calculation:

$$3,700,000,000 \times 365 \times 24 \times 60 \ \{= \# \text{ seconds}\}$$
$$\times \ 186,000 \ \{=C \ [\text{speed of light} \ / \ \text{second}]\}$$

× 0.9 miles[6] {= red shift factor}

The answer, of course, is incredibly large, even larger when you consider that this calculation is a calculation of distance. In order to arrive at a calculation of area, it needs to be extrapolated that the universe over the 3,700 million years was expanding in all directions.

If the simple $L \times H \times W$ basis were applied, the result would be:

3,700,000,000 × 365 × 24 × 60 {= # seconds}
× 186,000 {= C [speed of light/second]}
× 0.9 miles {= red shift factor}
times
3,700,000,000 × 365 × 24 × 60 {= # seconds}
× 186,000 {= C [speed of light / second]}
× 0.9 miles {= red shift factor}
times
3,700,000,000 × 365 × 24 × 60 {= # seconds}
× 186,000 {= C [speed of light / second]}
× 0.9 miles {= red shift factor}

The formula itself is large enough to be pasted to an internal wall and used as wallpaper; the result can be used to provide an exterior cover to a small dwelling.

Our nano U_1 now has some accurate dimensions, corrected to the nanometre.

This then concludes our current discussion regarding U_1 however the central point of this particular discussion was the fourteenth state, or a *singularity*, which is nano-sized.

---

[6] This figure of 90 per cent of light speed is taken as one of the redshift measures provided in *Companion to the Cosmos* by J. Gribbin (Weidenfield & Nicholson: London, 1986), p. 344.

Something Nebulous

Nebula: (*n.*) a gaseous mass or star cluster in the sky appearing as a hazy patch of light[7]

Nebulous: (*adj.*) indistinct, formless[8]

It can be suggested that the first of these definitions (should consistency be applied) can be regarded as a state. Had the idea of super states not been considered inappropriate, then a nebula is, of course, on a scale that could potentially qualify as such.

However this book is not intended to be a definitive guide to what can be considered as all states. It is a litmus test to ascertain whether the usage of states is an acceptable idea.

What is about to be done is to apply the idea of a thing to states, and with the simple notion that as space-time unfolds and events transpire, all things that occur obtain a state of existence.

Existence was not, and even though it has been cited as a state, it is not intended to be added to the list of states recorded thus far. The intention of this section is to create an element. The element having being denoted by the symbol Nb which stands for nebulobulim.

The fifteenth state therefore is nebulobulim.

Nebulobulim is an interesting element in that it is nebulous. The advantage of non-science in comparison to science is that elements can be considered to exist without the usual rigours being applied.

Let us then use some non-scientific means to discuss nebulobulim.

Con. 5: Nebulobulim is virtually undetectable.

Con. 6: Nebulobulim is a near-infinite resource

---

[7]   Gordon and Geddes, *English Dictionary* (Gordon & Geddes: Glasgow, 2010) p. 289.

[8]   Ibid.

Con. 7: Nebulobulim can be converted, should the means be available, into any other element of elementary-based object.

The question is whether or not these points of conjecture can be supported. Of course, science requires evidentiary support; however non-science (not wanting to be complete nonsense) shall at least adopt a rudimentary basis for this.

The answer lies buried somewhere in the Sinai.

This statement sounds like the type of statement found on an item of parchment buried in an urn in a remote cave for millennia.

Figure 15 depicts a haystack. What we are looking for, like those who try to follow the message in that urn, is the proverbial needle in a haystack.

The question is how to find it.

Figure 15: A haystack.

There is, of course, an interesting chain of events that occurred in the Sinai desert when bread fell from the sky. The question is how was it made and what was it made out of?

In addition to this, there is the question of what the universe itself was initially created from.

Nothing.

Can you create something from nothing, or must there have been something there in the first place?

In

...

Ti

The question can be asked why it was assumed that nebulobulim was a near-infinite material.

The answer is that the palette is notionally infinite hence the supply of nebulobulim, by definition, is also notionally infinite. Of course the estimate of the available supply of Nb using the simple assumption that U_1 is the only universe can be calculated as:

∞ – 3,700,000,000 × 365 × 24 × 60 {= # seconds}

× 186,000 {= C [speed of light / second]}

× 0.9 miles {= red shift factor} times

3,700,000,000 × 365 × 24 × 60 {= # seconds}

× 186,000 {= C [speed of light / second]}

× 0.9 miles {= red shift factor} times

3,700,000,000 × 365 × 24 × 60 {= # seconds}

× 186,000 {= C [speed of light / second]}

× 0.9 miles {= red shift factor}

The next issue to be resolved regards the detectability of nebulobulim. The answer that is simplest is that to date nothing has detected it; however the more interesting answer is that if nebulobulim as a material characteristic transforms itself, anything that detects it will be transformed from nebulobulim into the detectable basis.

It is like a chameleon.

There is one other matter to be discussed prior to finalising discussions regarding nebulobulim. Prior to this a further palette shall introduce another workspace, a planet.

Planets are complex bodies that usually orbit other bodies in the universe. Planets are comprised of matter—simplistically, solids, liquids, and gases. As a complex aggregation of matter, they can be considered like those other initial super states as items to be listed as states. However, for the same reason as nebulae this will not be the case.

The planetary palette includes some aspects of the planet within universe U_1 that are similar to planet E_1. One distinct difference is the lack of ice at the upper and lower extremities.

Are these important?

They are important ecologically to planet E_1 and analogously important to our discussion. The reason for this is that our original assumptions regarding the estimated size of universe U_1 require a slight alteration. The amount of this alteration is what this next section shall attempt to quantify.

> Con. 8: The universe U_1, at its inception, gained a certain amount of momentum across infinite space.

> Con. 9: Universe U_1 is copied or rendered as a copy via the element nebulobulim as it moves across infinite space.

These items of conjecture create a sort of time machine as the universe traverses infinite space and is copied. Those who can travel backwards through the infinite space that U_1 or any other universe has crossed, are able to view events of the past.

There are many questions regarding such matters however as this document is to precis states, they shall not be discussed in depth. One item of importance though is, how fast will you need to travel to traverse the time machine?

The initial estimation of the size of universe U_1 was a notional 30 per cent of its age. It had the following dimensions:

3,700,000,000 × 365 × 24 × 60 {= # seconds}
× 186,000 {= C [speed of light / second]} × 0.9 miles {=
red shift factor} miles

The estimated final size of universe U_1, considering constant rates of expansion, will increase to:

3,700,000,000 × 365 × 24 × 60 {= # seconds}
× 186,000 {= C [speed of light / second]}
× 0.9 miles {= red shift factor} miles × 2.333·

There are a significant number of assumptions regarding this calculation; however, it provides a reasonable estimate for the purposes of this document.

Of course, in this stage, universe U_1 will have the appearance displayed in our next palette. It is stark, and the time notation T1.0 denotes that it is the end of the lifespan of universe U_1. Some would say that this is the end of time however time (as discussed) is a state, a multifaceted state, and while this would be the end of time in the sense of universe U_1 containing matter that was not completely decayed or compressed into singularities, it is not the end of time overall.

Will the universe U_1 continue to expand after it reaches this final age?

Con. 10: The universe U_1 will cease to expand due to gravitational affects after reaching mature age 1.0.

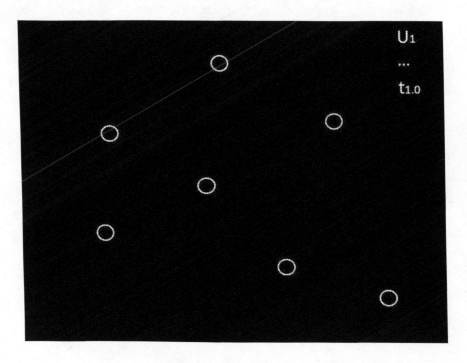

The light rings, of course, are simplistically artistic licence to represent decayed bodies that comprise U_1. They are lifeless, as universe U_1 itself.

Using the image and ecological oddity that are the icy regions at the extremities of planet E_1 a further assumption or item of conjecture can be stated prior to estimating the velocity through infinite space of universe U_1.

Con. 11: As the universe U_1 or any other universe is copied via nebulobulim as it traverses infinite space, then should the area that comprises that universe exceed its velocity through infinite space, it would result in the forming of crusts, like ice poles, to be known as *temporal encrustation*.

Our velocity for universe U_1 can now be estimated using the assumption of temporal encrustation. That is, the velocity through infinite space of universe U_1, based upon the estimated figures used within this document, is at a minimum:

3,700,000,000 × 365 × 24 × 60 {= # seconds}
× 186,000 {= C [speed of light / second]}
× 0.9 {= red shift factor} × 2.333· miles/second

Thus, the total volume of universe U_1 and availability of the infinite resource nebulobulim at age 0.3 of universe U_1 should be adjusted to:

3,700,000,000 × 365 × 24 × 60 × 186,000 {C} × 0.9 miles
times
3,700,000,000 × 365 × 24 × 60 × 186,000 {C} × 0.9 miles
times
3,700,000,000 × 365 × 24 × 60 × 186,000 {C} × 0.9 miles
times
3,700,000,000 × 365 × 24 × 60 × 186,000 {C} × 2.3333·
× 0.9 miles

The end result has not been calculated in full as the ten-digit calculator possessed by the author was unable to provide the figure. Those of you interested and possessing slightly larger calculators may attempt to derive the complete figure.

Interestingly Ert has found himself unable to remain completely involved in his other activities and at this point some Ertian ideas and corrections to the fallacious figure just calculated will be applied.

Ert has found himself a role as a performing clown with ice cream cone in hand, balancing upon a cylindrical drum as figure 16 illustrates. The cylinder is unlike the cube described and having its dimensions of length × height × width calculated.

Figure 16: Ert's cylindrical melodrama.

Cylinders are elongated circles rather than cubes, which are elongated rectangles. So the circular measure of $A = \pi r^2$ applies to calculating the volume of a cylinder.

Thus the formula calculating the size of the universe can be adjusted to accommodate Ert's view of the universe rather than the cubic expression provided.

However the idea of a cylindrical universe is better replaced by the idea of a conical universe, elongated at the rate calculated as the universal temporal velocity (UTV).

A cone has a radius that expands at a given rate rather than a cylinder, which has a constant diameter. Thus size of the universe can be calculated using an expanding algorithm once an expansion rate is ascertained.

The rudimentary cubic algorithm is sufficient to illustrate the intention of just how large the universe could conceptually be considered;

however, others more interested in mathematical accuracy may choose to try the conical or even the cylindrical computation.

Of interest and as a slight aside is that the speed calculated as the universal temporal velocity (UTV) of

$$3{,}700{,}000{,}000 \times 365 \times 24 \times 60 \times 186{,}000 \,\{C\} \times 2.3333$$
$$\times\ 0.9\ \text{miles/second}$$

is significantly greater than the speed of light (C) of 186,000 miles per second.

This enables nebulobulim to be discussed from a slightly different perspective. The initial palette that introduced infinite space was completely black. This was later altered to a range of colours on a light background with the introduction of nebulobulim.

What then is the colour and state of what exists outside the universe U_1?

Nebulobulim, as an element, is largely unknown in its properties; hence, it shall not be considered a state, although this can be argued. However, those familiar with automotive or other transport on planet E_1 will be familiar with the blurring effect on images as they pass a point where they are being captured on either an image-recording device or viewed by an indigenous inhabitant of E_1.

Of course, the significant estimated UTV of universe U_1 will mean that the inhabitants or recording devices of any sentient forms, such as those on E_1, will have difficulty accurately capturing an image of nebulobulim.

Nebulobulim, then, due to the issue of UTV speed, will (in addition to its chameleon like attributes) be difficult to record and view as per other even nano-sized objects where microscopic means are utilised.

This completes our discussion of the fifteenth state, nebulobulim.

The Genesis Factor

The sixteenth state is *God.*

Does God exist?

This is considered conjecture by some; however, using the simple basis of things, God exists in numerous forms. There are Egyptian, Greek, Roman, and myriad other gods that, as creations of the beings that inhabit planet E_1, all in fact exist.

The notion of things becomes important here in that there is a characteristic that things have when applied to species, such as those on E_1.

Self-fulfilling ideas.

Are there gods, and did these gods and can these gods affect the affairs of others? Of course, the idea was created by those who inhabit E_1 and affected their history and potentially could affect it again.

Things can be self-fulfilling ideas hence God would exist if those on E_1 had considered such to be the case.

What is of more interest though is figure 15. The haystack beyond the proverbial needle has another interesting property. A propensity in the right conditions to self-combust.

Spontaneous internal combustion.

Did U_1 form as the basis of some form of cosmic spontaneous internal combustion from nebulobulim, or was there some other cause?

The idea of God and the potential influence of some deity upon nebulobulim can be hinted at by some in a manner akin to our urn in the desert of the Sinai.

The sixteenth state then will have some interesting properties that some conjecture may assist in highlighting.

Con. 12: That the sixteenth state or God is sentient.

Con. 13: That the sixteenth state has an ability to affect or alter the fifteenth state or nebulobulim.

The ideas of omnipotence and omniscience derive from various groups regarding God as a separate entity to the Greek, Roman, or other forms. These are the simple basis of the application to the sixteenth state.

Penny for Your Thoughts

While it may seem to some that this is a sufficient introductory illustration of the notion of states, there is one last area that, in order to complete a crucial link, requires illustration.

The question of what (if any) link there is between the neuroverse and the universe is one that has been the subject of countless topics of discussion and debate in human history.

Shamanism spread its wings on the back of human consciousness and in the modern day has transcended itself and resurfaced as trance, meditation and many other forms of hypnotic or hallucinogenic substances, habits and institutions.

The human consciousness, awareness and the link between the notion of a sentient deity as mentioned in conjunction with the genesis factor and humanity pervades many parts of society.

This link though is of lesser importance to this topic than the more fundamental issue of matter.

The question is the human mind in part, named as the neuroverse, which encompasses both anatomical and fluctuational aspects of animal species, is what states exist (if any) in the fluctuational neuroverse?

Figure 16 is a magnetic image of a human brain and includes the so-called fluctuations. At this point the subject of this topic will address the question of states or matter. It is considered that there are two separate states. These are the following:

1. The seventeenth state is the memory.
2. The eighteenth state is thought.

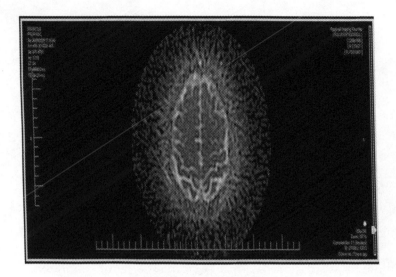

Figure 17: Mind over matter.

These have been divided into two as it is considered that, like the digital state stores data and also processes data, the neuroverse and in particular the mind behaves similarly.

A further quirky and fun thought is a little game a person may want to try regarding how the memory state functions. Is it entirely internal (i.e. stored within the brain cavity), or is it perhaps somehow linked to the wider universe through some quantum or other means?

Cast your mind back.

Have you ever been asked to do this?

How far did you get? Was it years?

If you want to calculate this as speed and time, calculate the length of time from when you started to recall how far back it was and how long it took.

Then use your speed calculator of

$$3{,}700{,}000{,}000 \times 365 \times 24 \times 60 \times 186{,}000 \,\{C\} \times 2.3333$$
$$\times\ 0.9 \text{ miles/second}$$

to estimate the distance you travelled.

What is interesting about the image in figure 17 is that the actual fluctuations have spread far beyond the cranium. This is of interest as it may assist in substantiating an item of conjecture.

> Con. 14: The human mind can interact with the broader universe and even other minds via telepathy, telekinesis or other like-termed means.

The link between thought and memory can best be illustrated analogously via a simple image.

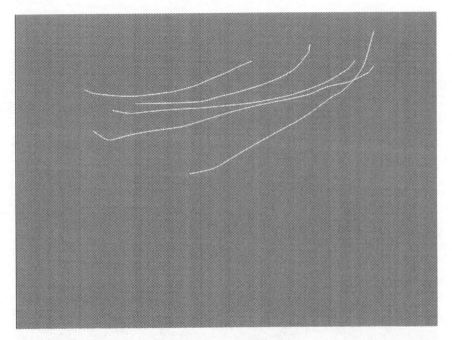

Figure 18: On a cloudy day.

Figure 18 is a simple illustration of an early cloud formation that you may have seen on many days that started with a clear blue sky.

Cirrus clouds.

These wispy streaks may develop as you lie on the ground and stare upwards into stratus, nimbus, cumulus, cumulo-stratus, or other combinations.

Thoughts from young ages extending into memories may be considered simplistically in the same way.

Can these structures be affected?

Yes. An example is the sportsperson or other person whose head impacts another object, causing them to become simply addled, concussed, or even worse.

Using this analogy, it can be conceived that a person's thoughts can be rearranged, as a cloud pattern is, via similar methods, although this will not be without peril.

What is of interest though is the link between the neuroverse and reality?

The question of who we are is in part the result of hard-coded or genetic behaviours and those learned via the accumulation of memories as per the cloud formation analogy.

Whether this can be altered is in part answered by the notion of rearranging those memories; however, there is another test—reality rules.

Reality rules measure the impact an event has on resultant behaviour. For instance, an event may lead to thoughts of elation, perhaps depression, or even loathing. The measure of this behavioural impact on an individual after an event is known as *reality rules*.

Of course people can cover or behaviourally modify their reactions; however this cannot be sustained under close scrutiny. The underlying behavioural basis can be observed by a trained person.

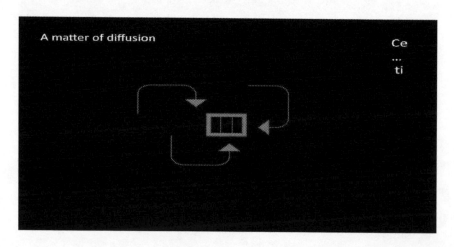

The previous page represents what may be considered a departure from the topic being discussed. The palette is a cellular workspace. The cell represents, in this instance a body enlarged like the nano in previous palettes.

Cells are present in all livings things and are microscopic in size. Within the structure that is depicted as fluid, like in our palette, are numerous structures and compounds. Cells can be considered super states or states according to this analysis. However, as with other items they will not be included within the list as they are not central to the scope of this particular body of work.

Of note are the lines of entry or structures that are on the external face of the cell. These are to indicate that cells, like rooms or buildings, are not separated totally from the external world.

The use of the cell is to allow an analysis of how the mind and universe interact as per previous discussions. The cellular palette has a fluid centre, as water, used as the basis of depicting the early states of liquid, solid, and gas and has an interesting property.

When distributed unevenly water will migrate to equalise its molecular distribution in a process known as osmosis.

In the instance of the cellular palette, water will move into the cell via the membranes marked with white apertures via what is termed osmotic pressure.

The mind, or brain, may analogously be viewed as interacting with the external universe in a similar manner. The picture in figure 17 and the emotional state palette both depict how the brain and brain waves function.

The universe as noted in the discussion of transmissions as a state, can be viewed similarly. As such there is an interaction as per the osmotic basis of water between the universe and the mind.

Those familiar with the *Star Wars* film and other literature may remember the use of the Force as a tool of some members within that particular character set.

This interaction and the basis of how the mind may become unequalised or require equalising can be likened to changes in pressure being exerted akin to osmotic pressure. Concentration, or the act of concentrating, is of course the reverse, where the mind exerts pressure externally. Osmosis works in a similar manner and may in the cellular world move internally or externally.

This concludes the discussion of the neuroverse and the two states:

1. memory
2. thought.

Thus

This section of our discussion provided much more of the basis of non-science. Whether or not it is nonsense is something that those who read the detail and attempt to apply it will judge.

The initial basis of considering matter and using the term of *states* as a means of classification was returned to after the discussion of super states.

This dichotomy of states and super states remains and is referred to once again in this section. However, even super states are, for the purposes of consistency, regarded as states. Of greater significance was the number of other entities, such as nebula, that were referred to (yet not classified as) a state.

This is due to the fact that this is a conceptual discussion, and while at this juncture the notion of using states seems useful to the writer, it may not to others, or perhaps there is an existing system.

IN CONCLUSION

The question of whether, or where, non-science progresses beyond this point can only be considered speculation. Non-science by its very nature is speculative so this seems consistent.

States and the use of this logical method of classification seem to have application, at least to the writer. In addition to this there were some extremely speculative mathematical equations. All this is an extrapolation of the initial ideas that gave impetus to this book.

Prior to its completion there is one last workspace that shall be displayed. It is to conceptualise greater space and provide some basis for speculation outside the scope of this book that is possibly in line with the thinking of others.

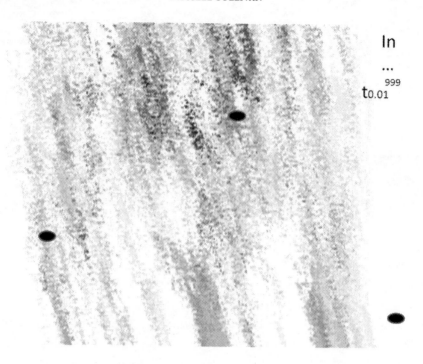

There is, the image of U_1 as a desolate, lifeless entity at $t1.0$. This in some ways likens the existence of a universe as an entity to that described for entities in the digital state, transient. While U_1 has existed for the 3.7 billion years estimated it has a finite life and, like those binary figures that underpin the digital state will expire to the extent of having an energy signature at the end of its life.

What else then?

The infinite palette is infinite, a potentially slinky trail lithe and nubile as a cat, U_2, U_3, etc., will unfold or unfurl. This is one of myriad possibilities.

Does it matter? Possibly not. However it is grounds for thought. That concludes the discussion of non-science with a splash of colour and a dose of conjecture.

A Deduction

The following was not part of the completed *The Book of Things*. It was added not as an afterthought but as a method to enable segues between this book and others. That was erroneous, and fortunately, *The Book of Things* was not published with this included.

What is more fortunate is that *The Book of Things*, as a conclusion, added a deduction.

Nascence

Do you have a sense of smell?

Something is very fishy about this book. Its nonsensical non-science. The intuitive aspect of our self, our id, is our internal sense of smell. Our logical olfactory system.

To place the details of this book in context, we will take the process or state of nascence to define all that is contained within these pages.

It is said that nature can be summarised into three basic forms. These being:

1. animal
2. vegetable
3. mineral.

Like our three states this system of classification is derived from science taught during my early school science. From those lessons, my interest was piqued by two markers, markers being factors or entities that would identify or ID a particular item. These markers were:

1. Rh: The rhesus factor derived from a species of monkey that enabled blood and blood products to be specifically analysed and utilised. This factor is positive (+) and negative (–) yet able to be paired with a grouping of O to be given a neutral basis.

2. Ph: Ph is the litmus test of life in plants. Phosphates, which are used in compounds such as urea, form complex chains, enabling vegetable life to flourish while interestingly being used in the form of tests known as Ph tests to find and define balance and imbalance.

What then of the mineral?

Animals and vegetables have complex systems that enable and, indeed, require complex and common markers in different guises to enable them to function.

Minerals, though, simplistically are dormant, lifeless, dull!

One of the great rivers of Earth is so vast that it covers an entire continent. This is Antarctica, and the Ross Sea and Ross Ice Shelf are one of many features that link to this vast river of ice.

Another great river flows regularly from the sides of Kilauea in Hawaii. This is a river of ice that, from magma far beneath our earth's crust, vents its frustration at being hemmed in like jam in a sandwich in many different forms.

When one thinks of minerals perhaps gemstones (with the lustrous wonder of diamonds), silicates (whose abundance makes them wondrous), or carbons (which are so basic to animals and minerals) spring to mind.

Markers such as Rh and Ph were found via analysis of both animals and vegetables. Minerals—such as those diamonds, silicates, and carbons—perhaps through analysis could yield something similar.

What then of fire and ice?

Our rivers themselves like the tributaries that carry the Rh factor and deliver Ph are they mineral?

Commonality of a nonsensical non-science nature termed Nh shall be attributed to the mineral world.

Nascence.

Formative in its nature nascence represents the perspective upon which this form of non-science can be best construed by others. The states in which minerals find themselves are nascent, changing and changeable, moving to the ebb, and flow of time and the forces of nature, similar to the state of the non-science that comprises this text.

In Summary

It is possible, after discussing nascence to become specist—that is, to rank animal, vegetable, mineral in that order. This, of course, follows much doctrine; however it will lead to a potential oversight.

If Nh as a notion was considered to be a marker in the mineral world, or mineral state, it could follow that it would also be a marker in the vegetable and mineral states.

Minerals form the basis of vegetables and animals.

The potential also for states to be reconsidered or considered differently from our conceptual starting point of gas, liquid, and solid is also highlighted in this analysis. The landscape of states, then, is considered nascent and as the starting point can be viewed and reviewed from different perspectives, potentially always nascent.

This is not considered a weakness in this text simply a way of highlighting how nothing more complex than perspective can give rise to ideas that differ from the norm.

Non-science was described as nonsense at the outset to highlight this and to ensure that science in its 'proper' form was recognised. Is there a place for non-science?

It is believed so, and it is hoped that this in some small way, may contribute to that which is science and that those who study or simply have their interest piqued in the simple questions of what, where or why will find some value in what has been attempted in these pages.

In closing, it must be remembered that *The Book of Things* has established non-science or nonsense as the basis of PAUONH exposition. Science and scientific method work towards certainty, knowledge, and understanding. This is why science is seen as benefactorial and has contributed much.

A novel entitled *Target 382* is now in progress and may never reach its completion, this simply being beyond the written skills of me as an author. It is a remnant, a fraction until complete. Those who dabble in space may giggle at my introduction of a sub-traction machine to navigate the byways of the cosmos.

Knowledge creates certainty; certainty creates comfort, yet PAUONH has shunned this.

Why?

There is now perhaps a palatable answer. Deduction is a positive; it adds. And science and certainty remove deduction in essence, as part of the greater whole they become negatives. It is deduction, the negative, that creates the ability to open doors, debate and form conjecture.

Deduction is the art of conjecture, and it was that which the writer unknowingly had lost. *The Book of Things* shuns certainty yet it has filled the gap in its writer's self.

EPILOGUE

There are many issues with this book, not the least that for the most part it is nonsense. Of particular concern or interest to some may be the issue of depth or level of detail.

It may be said that it discusses at a level that is no more than skin-deep. That is so and was the intention from the outset. So as a fitting conclusion, here is a small piece of text that is entitled 'Skin-Deep'.

Skin-Deep

Glistening smile shimmered bright
Lake upon a moonlit night
Teeth did glow, and eyes did glare
Skin-deep the waters of despair

Upon a rock, a monkey sat
Put on its head wide-brimmed hat
Chittering madly, nobody there
Skin-deep, a mind unaware

Twinkle star, night-time sky
Dragon's breath, luminescent eye
Underneath an igneous dome
Skin-deep, phallus no aplomb

Water cast your waves astray
Those amidst foundering way
Arthur's gone; Excalibur lost
Skin-deep tales nobly told

Put a penny in a well
Take it out, make your wealth
Find another golden spoil
Skin-deep, fabulous wishes gone

Thinly spread
Lightly trod
Little there
Skin-deep

Twist your hair in a plait
Curly tail, piglet squeal
Cross the road of desire
Skin-deep, lusting hearts afire

Not enough
Little done
Subtle lines
Nimbly drawn

Turn the page
Read another
Skin-deep level
But sufficient

APPENDICES

Summary of Conjectures

Number	Conjecture
1	The arrangements of matter depicted within this section are broad enough to encapsulate what science would describe at this point in time.
2	The universe U_1 is the first universe to contain sentient life; hence, it is so numerically depicted.
3	For the purposes of estimation in non-science, the universe U1 will be considered not two-dimensional, or planar, but three-dimensional.
4	For the purposes of estimation on non-science, a cubic shape, rather than cylindrical or other solid object shape, shall be assumed.
5	Nebulobulim is virtually undetectable.
6	Nebulobulim is a near-infinite resource
7	Nebulobulim can be converted, should the means be available, into any other element of elementary-based object.
8	The universe U_1, at its inception gained a certain amount of momentum across infinite space.

Number	Conjecture
9	Universe U_1 is copied or rendered as a copy via the element nebulobulim as it moves across infinite space.
10	The universe U_1 will cease to expand due to gravitational affects after reaching mature age 1.0.
11	As the universe U_1 or any other universe is copied via nebulobulim as it traverses infinite space, then should the area that comprises that universe exceed its velocity through infinite space it would result in the forming of crusts, like ice poles, to be known as *temporal encrustation*.
12	The sixteenth state has an ability to affect or alter the fifteenth state or nebulobulim.
13	That the sixteenth state or God is sentient.
14	That the human mind can interact with the broader universe and even other minds via telepathy, telekinesis or other like-termed means.

Listing of States

Name	Identification
solids	the first state
liquids	the second state
gases	the third state
transmissions	the fourth state
particles	the fifth state
time	the sixth state
money	the seventh state
digitisation	the eighth state
quantum	the ninth state

Name	Identification
nature	the tenth state
emotion	the eleventh state
reality	the twelfth state
state	the thirteenth state
singularity	the fourteenth state
nebulobulim	the fifteenth state
God	the sixteenth state
memory	the seventeenth state
thought	the eighteenth state

Table of Symbols

Symbol	Name	Symbol	Name
In ...	infinite workspace	Mo ...	molecular workspace
∞ ...	infinite workspace	Te ...	temporal workspace
Fi ...	financial workspace	Di ...	digital workspace
Qu ...	quantum workspace	Nt ...	natural workspace
Em ...	emotional workspace	Re ...	reality workspace
St ...	state workspace	Pl ...	planetary workspace
Ce ...	cellular workspace		
a	arbitrary	i	irrelevant
e	estimated	u	unknown

Table of Conversions

Conversion ratios quoted within this book are listed to enable verification or application of any formulae is provided below.

Measurement	Equivalent
1 mile	1,600 metres
1 year	365 days
1 light metre/second	186,000 × 1,600

Table of Elements

Elements cited within this text are listed below to enable verification.

Abbreviation	Element
H_2O	Water
Na	Sodium
Nb	Nebulobulim
Nh	that which is nascent, elemental to all things, a marker potentially non-existent, making it all the more remarkable in its all-encompassing form

BIBLIOGRAPHY

Bills of Exchange Act (Australian Parliament, 1908).

Geddes and Grosset, *English Dictionary* (Geddes & Grosset: Glasgow, 2010).

Greene, B, *The Elegant Universe* (Vintage: London, 2005).

Gribbin, J., *Companion to the Cosmos* (Weidenfeld and Nicholson: London, 1996).

Sullivan, R., *A Question of Intelligence: Updated for Reappraisal* (PAUONH: Melbourne, 2012).

GLOSSARY

Terms and definitions that do not necessarily conform with standard usage are defined below.

Term	Definition
transience	Temporary existence and temporarily existent states.
visual acuity factor	A degree of increase in the size of a microscopic object to enable viewing without the aid of microscopic or other enhancing equipment.
temporal encrustation	A formation of matter at the extremities of a universe through the transformation of nebulobulim should that universe have a temporal velocity less than its width at that point in time.
temporal velocity	The velocity of a universe through infinite space.
universal temporal velocity (UTV)	The velocity at which a universe progresses across infinite space.
reality rules	Measures the impact an event has on resultant behaviour. For instance, an event may lead to thoughts of elation, perhaps depression or even loathing.

Printed in the United States
By Bookmasters